MW01622176

Thekla Verlag

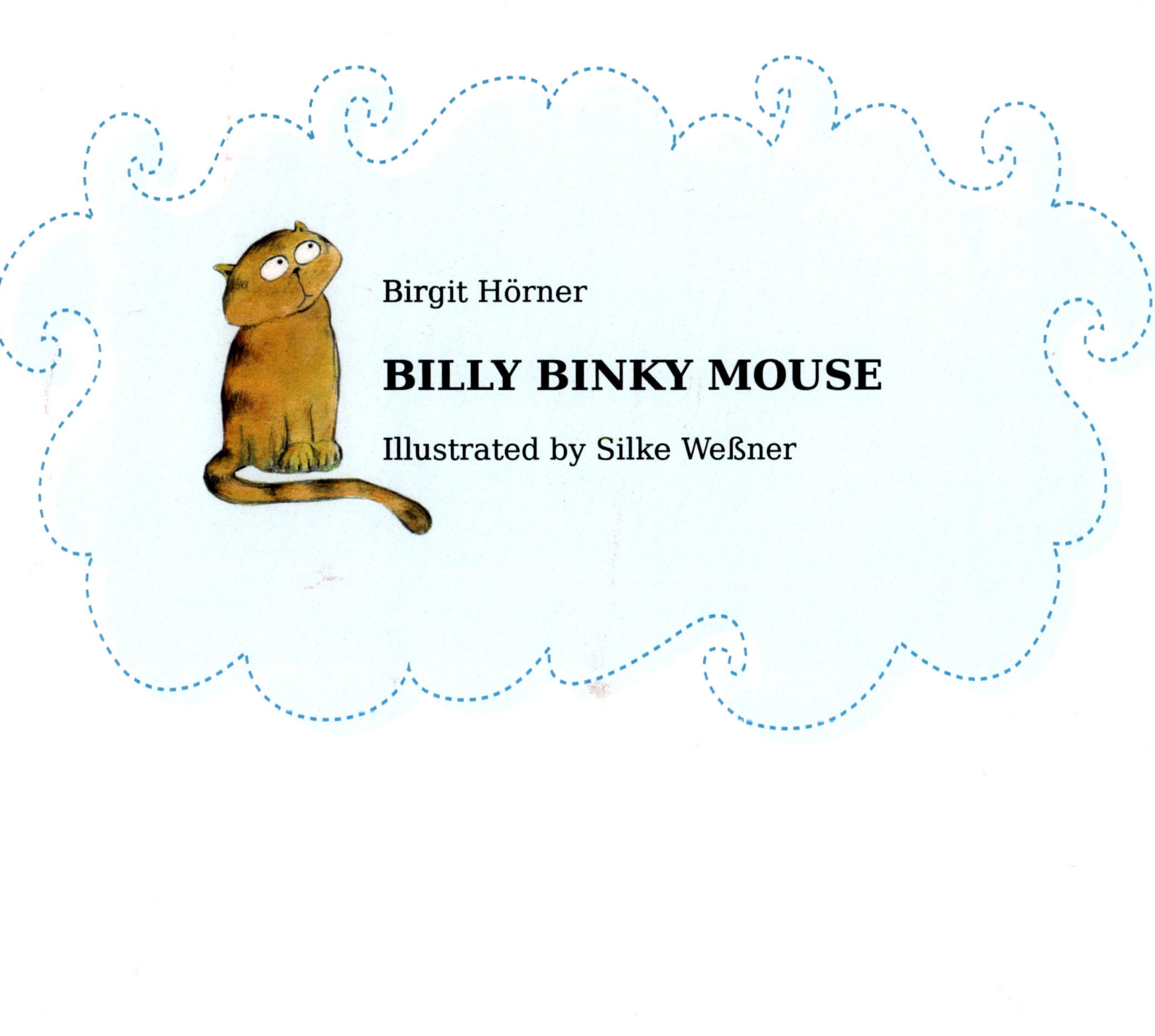

Birgit Hörner

BILLY BINKY MOUSE

Illustrated by Silke Weßner

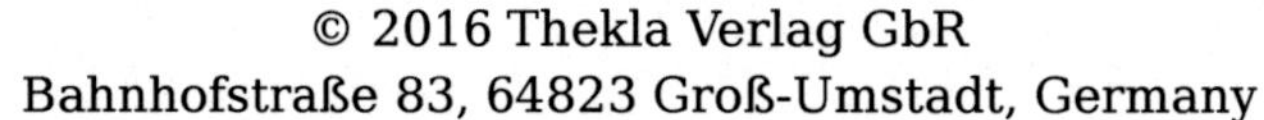

Bahnhofstraße 83, 64823 Groß-Umstadt, Germany

ISBN 978-3-945711-10-1 (Softcover)

also available as an e-book:
ISBN 978-3-945711-11-8 (kindle Edition)

Original title: Klaus Schnullermaus,
first published in German language
(ISBN 978-3-945711-01-9, Hardcover)
in Germany 2014 by Thekla Verlag GbR.

1st English Edition, 2016

www.thekla-verlag.de

FOR OUR SONS:

Paul, Cham and Emil. Jonas, Joshua and Finn.

Do you love binkies? Do you need your binky when you're sad or hurt? Or if you are really upset? To snuggle up or to fall asleep?

I can relate because that's just how I feel! I am totally crazy about binkies! I gather them wherever I can. And when I hear about a child that will soon be old enough to sleep without his binky, I secretly sneak into the house.

Oh my gosh! Did I really forget to introduce myself?

My name is Billy Binky Mouse. But don't be scared: I would never steal your binkies, honestly. I just want to offer you a trade. In my backpack I carry presents for big kids who are ready to give me their binky in exchange. Maybe I can come and visit you someday.

But for today, I'm going to visit Peter's house. He is quite a big boy already. Actually, he doesn't want to give his binkies away yet, but his Mom says it's about time to get along without them.

What do you think? Will Peter make it?

This is Peter. Peter always keeps his binkies close at hand. He takes them with him everywhere he goes. Sometimes even to the soccer field, because Peter loves playing soccer almost as much as he loves his binkies.

Peter says, »You never know when you need one!«

Look! This is where Peter lives. It is a nice red house with lots of windows and a beautiful garden. Do you think Billy will find a hole to sneak in? Let's see.

Oh, I'll make it into the house! I'm Billy Binky Mouse!

The whole family is at the table for dinner. Big Peter, little Ida, Mommy and Daddy. Peter and Ida are already in their pj's. It's bedtime soon.
But where are Peter's binkies?!

Oh, let's take a quick sneak into Peter's bedroom
before the family is done with dinner.
By chance I'll find Peter's binkies.

Oh shoot! Pumpkin the
fat cat is sleeping right beside the door.
Be quiet, Billy! Tiptoe, don't wake the cat!

Look, there is Ida's crib! Her little, pink binkies smell so sweet that Billy needs to snuffle, just a little. Billy Binky Mouse knows: Ida is still a little girl. She needs her binkies.

Peter has also taken his binkies to his bedroom. They are all there: Pirate-binky, the green one, the red one, the yellow one with the sun and the blue binky with the teddy bear.

Riddle, criddle, play,
I'll just take one away.
Binky Billy's in the house.
Now, isn't he a clever mouse?

Listen, Billy! Somebody's coming! Hurry up.
Quick, hide inside Peter's toy-castle!

»Mommy! My green binky is gone! Where can it be?«

Peter is really upset. He is searching everywhere.

»Did you take my green binky, Ida?«

But Ida didn't take Peter's binky. She's got her own binkies.

»Did you take my green binky, Pumpkin?«

But Pumpkin didn't take Peter's binky either.

He is sleeping and dreaming of fat mice.

Mommy ponders.

»You know what I think, honey? It's about time! You are a big boy now. I believe Billy Binky Mouse is in the house.«

Peter takes his red binky and puts it in his mouth.

»That's okay. Still got one!« he says.

And indeed that is true: Billy Binky Mouse is in the house. And he has got a present for Peter in his backpack.

Peter is sleeping tight.
Very quiet, on tippy toes,
I'll snatch another binky.
Maybe the red one?

Riddle, criddle, play,
I'll just take one away.
Which one to take today?
The red one I would say.

The next morning Peter climbs down the stairs excitedly.

»Listen everyone! Now my red binky is gone, too! We have to catch this stupid mouse so he can't take my other binkies! Everybody has to help! Also Pumpkin, because he is a good mice hunter.«

The whole family searches. They search everywhere.

Daddy searches in the car.

Ida searches in the toy box.

Peter even searches inside the washing machine.

Pumpkin searches underneath the bed.

Mommy searches between the books.

But they can't find Billy Binky Mouse anywhere. He is hiding too good.

Oh, oh, that was close! Pumpkin the cat almost caught me. So, while everybody is busy looking for me downstairs, I'll take the chance and sneak into Peter's bedroom again.

There they are, Pirate-binky, the yellow one with the sun, and the blue binky with the teddy bear – Peter hid them all under his pillow.

Riddle, criddle, play,
I'll take one more away.
Which one can he bear?
I know, the teddy bear.

Peter is upset. Billy Binky Mouse is still in the house. Even Pumpkin wasn't able to find him. But to be honest, Pumpkin sleeps all the time. And now also the blue binky with the teddy bear is gone.

»Well, that's okay. Still got one!«
Peter says.

Peter puts the yellow binky with the sun in his mouth and firmly closes his hand around his Pirate-binky when going to bed.

He wakes Pumpkin, who is fast asleep at his bedside, and demands,

»Pumpkin! You watch out and chase Billy Binky Mouse away when he comes!«

Billy Binky Mouse is still in the house. Peter is asleep and snoring softly. Pirate-binky is still safe in his hand, but where is the yellow one with the sun? Is Pumpkin really watching out for the mouse?

Be quiet, Billy! Tiptoe! Don’t wake the cat!

RIDDLE, CRIDDLE, PLAY,
I'LL TAKE ONE MORE AWAY.
I'LL SNITCH THE BINKY WITH THE SUN,
IF PETER WAKES, I'LL CUT AND RUN.

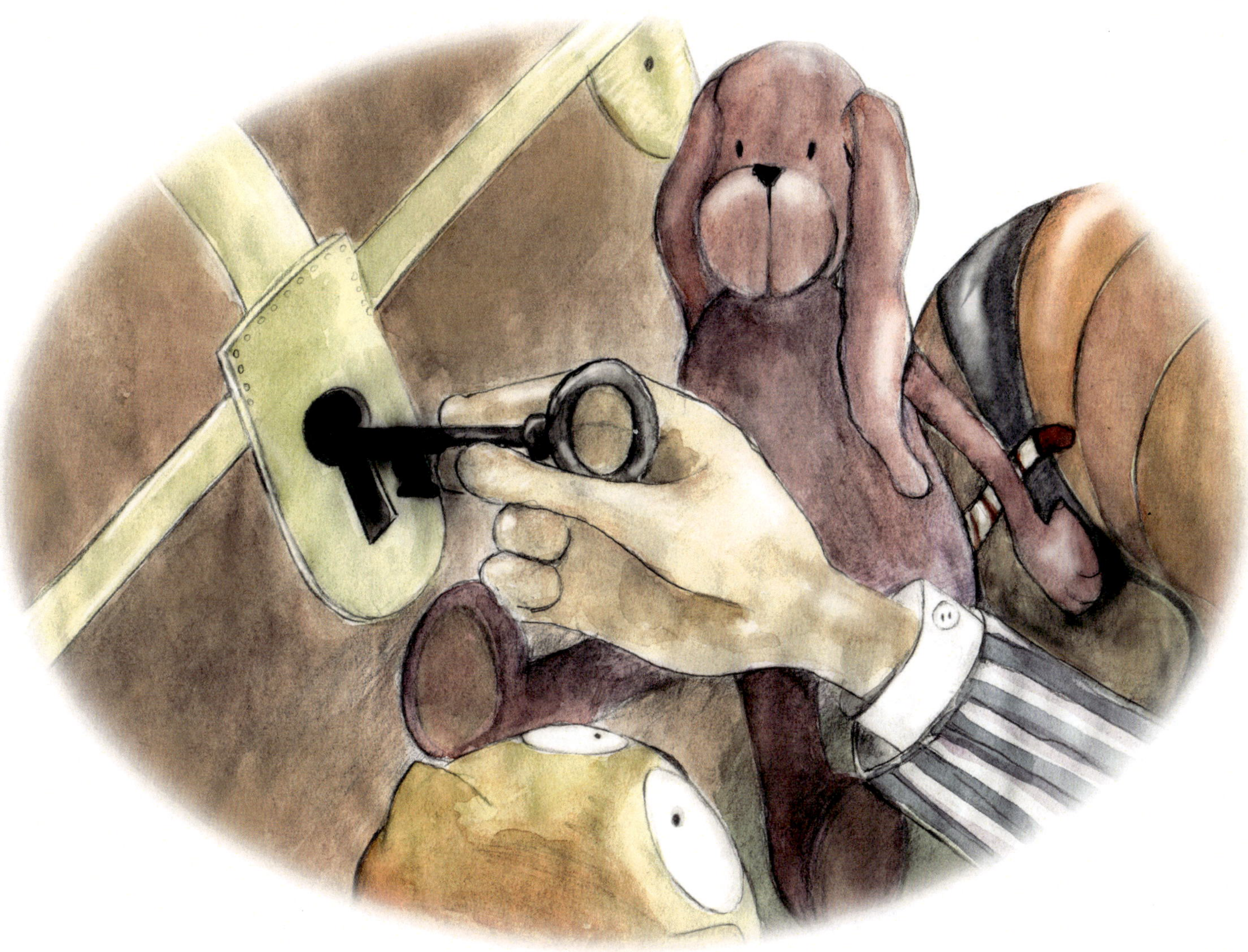

Now Pirate-binky is the only one left. Pumpkin is trying to comfort Peter. Unfortunately he fell asleep again and didn't notice Billy Binky Mouse sneaking into Peter's room last night.

Today Peter doesn't want to take a risk. He puts his last binky in his treasure chest and locks it tightly. It should be safe in there.

I am Billy Binky Mouse and I'm still in the house.
Tiny as I am, I fit through every hole.

Uhhh, it is quite dark in here!

Ah, there the binky is!

Riddle, criddle, play,
this last one I won't take away.
Now for tonight,
I'll just take a little bite.

Peter keeps his last binky inside his treasure chest until bedtime. But what is this? Someone seems to have nibbled away two little pieces.

Mommy tucks Peter into bed and Peter takes his last broken binky in his mouth.

»Doesn't work anymore!« Peter shouts angrily and throws Pirate-binky out of bed.

Mommy cuddles Peter and stays at his bedside to comfort him until he falls asleep.

When Peter wakes up the next morning, he is very proud of himself. The whole night he slept without any binky. Now, he really is a big boy! He draws a picture of a soccer ball and leaves it together with Pirate-binky on the carpet for Billy Binky Mouse.

»Trade binky for soccer ball!« Peter shouts out loudly, so that Billy Binky Mouse certainly hears him.

»Trade soccer ball for binky!«
Billy Binky Mouse whispers from out
of his secret hiding place.

Bye-bye big Peter, bye-bye little Ida.

Bye Mommy, bye Daddy and bye-bye Pumpkin.

I'll be back as soon as Ida is a big girl.

Instructions for Parents

THIS IS HOW IT WORKS:

Make sure that in the beginning your child has got numerous pacifiers on hand to make it possible for you to let them disappear slowly, one by one.

Take away one pacifier each day.

Every evening sit down with your child and count the remaining ones. Comfort your child and make plans how to catch or scare away the stupid mouse.

Prepare yourself and your child for the day that the last binky will be gone. Talk to your child about the present that Billy Binky Mouse will bring in exchange for the last pacifier. Encourage your child to draw a picture of the present and put it out for the mouse. At the best case you can convince your child to give up the last pacifier by its own choice. If this doesn't work, it is up to you to also »steal« away the last pacifier.

Make no other plans for this special evening, you should have enough time to console your child for its big loss. Snuggle and sing your child to sleep and be there during the night in case it wakes up again.

Probably it is going to be as hard for you as for your child to take this last step. But: Be patient and consistent.

Once your child has managed the first night without the pacifier, it must be rewarded immediately with the present from Billy Binky Mouse.

If you as a parent manage to be consistent and stand by your decision, your child will very soon be able to sleep without a pacifier.

For more information on Billy Binky Mouse and pacifier weaning visit **www.billy-binky-mouse.com**

Grab your colored pencils!

Pumpkin and Billy Binky Mouse are waiting for you to color them in!

Made in the USA
San Bernardino, CA
08 June 2017